OLD EDINBURGH TRAMS

KENNETH G. WILLIAMSON

AMBERLEY

First published 2019

Amberley Publishing
The Hill, Stroud
Gloucestershire, GL5 4EP

www.amberley-books.com

Copyright © Kenneth G. Williamson, 2019

The right of Kenneth G. Williamson to be identified
as the Author of this work has been asserted in
accordance with the Copyrights, Designs and
Patents Act 1988.

ISBN 978 1 4456 9553 2
E-BOOK ISBN 978 1 4456 9554 9

British Library Cataloguing in Publication Data.
A catalogue record for this book is available from
the British Library.

Typeset in 9.5pt on 12pt Celeste.
Origination by Amberley Publishing.
Printed in the UK.

Introduction

The first trams to run in Edinburgh were horse-drawn and were operated by the Edinburgh Street Tramways Company. The inaugural service (Haymarket to Bernard Street in Leith) started on 6 November 1871. Horse trams were soon extended to serve the then extent of the city and the separate Burgh of Leith. However, the streets immediately to the north of the 'New Town' were too steep to be served by horse traction, namely Hanover/Dundas Streets and Frederick/Howe Streets, with gradients of up to 1 in 11.

To serve these exceptionally steep routes, in January 1888 the Edinburgh Northern Tramways Company started a cable-hauled tram service firstly from Hanover Street to Goldenacre (based on the technology used by the San Francisco cable car system). In February 1890 the Frederick Street to Comely Bank route was opened. Both routes were served by a depot and power house at 57 Henderson Row, Edinburgh, with a single track connection to each. This depot, after cable traction ceased, became a police garage and more recently was demolished to build the offices of the Royal London Financial Institution. During construction, pulleys from the cable days were uncovered and one set was incorporated in the side of the building with an explanatory plaque about the history of the site.

These two routes were most successful and this led Edinburgh Council to decide to convert all the horse tram routes to the cable system, which then involved the intricacy of cables serving complex city junctions. They were also swayed by the fact that, unlike electric trams, no obtrusive overhead poles and wires would be required to be erected in Princes Street. Thus, the cable trams spread throughout Edinburgh from October 1899 to 1908.

Leith Corporation would not countenance cable haulage within its Burgh and purchased the horse-drawn Leith tramlines from Edinburgh Street Tramways in 1904 and, in 1905, introduced electric traction. The fleet livery was Munich lake and ivory. This lack of agreement between the two local authorities led to through-running from Edinburgh to Leith being impossible, requiring a change of vehicle from cable to electric at the Burgh boundaries at Pilrig Street junction with Leith Walk. Inevitably this arrangement was very unpopular with passengers and caused the situation to be dubbed 'the Pilrig Muddle'.

The First World War was the beginning of the end for the cable system in Edinburgh. Many of the skilled drivers and maintenance staff were in the armed services, their absence causing deterioration to the complex installation of the system, which lead to many faults and severe delays to tram services. This could not go on and the Corporation took over the system on 1 July 1919, creating Edinburgh Corporation Tramways Department with the remit of converting all the routes to electric traction. They opted for four-wheeled double-deck trams painted dark red (madder) and white – a livery still used by Lothian Buses and Edinburgh's new trams. Edinburgh Corporation Tramways Department took over the Leith system on 10 November 1920, when the Burghs of Leith and Edinburgh merged, thus allowing (at last) a through service on Leith Walk. This was accomplished in June 1922 and the last cable car ran on the Portobello line in June 1923. A short section of original tram rail and cable track can still be seen in Waterloo Place.

In 1928, following the growing importance of buses, Edinburgh Corporation Tramways Department was renamed Edinburgh Corporation Transport Department.

The last Edinburgh trams ran on 16 November 1956. The main reason given for the switch to buses was the inflexibility of the tram routes, should problems occur (one accident could bring down the whole system). Strange then that many other cities worldwide kept, expanded, and modernised their tram systems.

The only Edinburgh electric tram preserved is No. 35, built in 1948. This was housed in a small museum at Shrubhill Depot. The museum closed in 1988 due to structural faults with the roof. Tram number 35 operated at the Glasgow Garden Festival in 1988 and on the Blackpool tramway. It is now at the National Tramway Museum in Crich, Derbyshire. There is an exceptionally well-restored horse car, No. 23, which was for many years a summerhouse in a Borders garden, and can now be seen at the Lathalmond Bus Museum in Fife. One of the 1903 built cable cars, No. 226, is presently being restored to open top condition, having been used as a holiday chalet also in the Borders from about 1938 to 1988.

Musselburgh had its own electrified tram system from 1904. Passengers had to change to the cable-hauled Edinburgh trams at Joppa until 1923, when cable operation finally ceased. The Musselburgh system was subsequently incorporated into the Edinburgh system, with the tramway to Port Seton which opened in 1909, closing east of Levenhall in 1928. Musselburgh was served by Edinburgh trams until 1954.

Trams returned to Edinburgh on 31 May 2014, under controversial circumstances, but have proved extremely popular with ridership well up on original estimations. There are plans to further extend the system. The modern tram differs quite considerably from the old trams, not only in appearance but in the many modern features they have, making them much more user friendly – no more jumping on and off the back of trams. The new trams also carry a lot more passengers compared to the old ones.

It remains to be seen whether or not the new trams will have the same love and affection the old trams had with the people of Edinburgh and Leith.

The introduction of trams in 1905 led to the decline and eventual closure to passengers of many of Leith's railway stations.

There were latterly four tram depots in Edinburgh and Leith: Gorgie, Leith, Portobello and Tollcross. In addition there were workshops at Shrubhill which built not only the original horse trams but also electric trams, as well as carrying out repairs and general maintenance. Shrubhill also acted as a depot from time to time.

The system continued to expand during the 1930s. New routes included Gorgie and Stenhouse (1930), Braids to Fairmilehead (1936) and North Gyle to Maybury (1937).

The war years did not have a great impact, apart from curtailing further extensions, on Edinburgh's trams and the system remained intact until 1950, when the opportunity was taken to provide a bus service to one of the new housing areas beyond the tram routes. Service 18 was withdrawn and replaced by a bus service, also numbered 18, which ran from Davidson's Mains to Burdiehouse. In June of 1950 a recommendation was accepted to scrap 25 per cent of the system. This involved the routes to Comely Bank, Stenhouse and Slateford. Withdrawal of the Comely Bank route was first in 1952. The others followed later that year and into 1953, by which time it had been agreed to scrap the remainder of the system.

The immediate post-Second World War years proved to be the busiest for the trams with a record number of nearly 193 million passengers being carried in 1947. Edinburgh took advantage of the closure of the Manchester system to purchase eleven modern second-hand trams numbered 401 to 411 between 1947 and 1949. Concurrently the last six electrified cable cars, and some of the 1922 batch of electric cars, were withdrawn.

The last Edinburgh trams ran on 16 November 1956 and finished with a parade led by a horse-drawn omnibus from the Mound down to Shrubhill Depot.

I have fond memories as a small boy of Leith Depot as my father, Henry (Harry) Vincent Fuller Williamson, was a tram driver and then a bus driver who worked out of Leith Depot. I can still recall the smell of stewed tea and bacon rolls whenever you entered the canteen.

My father was one of the first drivers of the then new One Man Operated (OMO) buses.

Every summer there was an ECT picnic to Alva with buses leaving from Smith's Place, just off Leith Walk, festooned with streamers and full of excited children. At Christmas there was a children's party held in Leith Depot which was also was great fun.

Map of the system – 1937–50

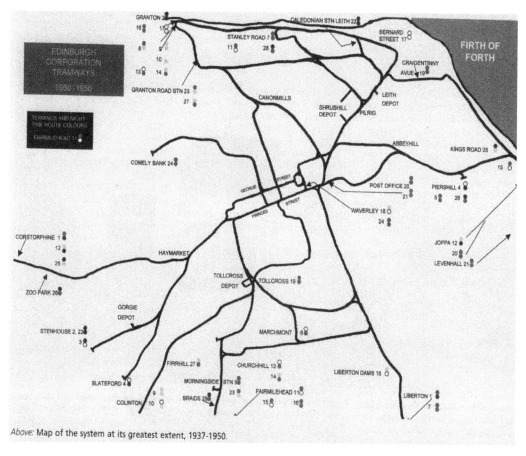

Above: Map of the system at its greatest extent, 1937-1950.

Gauge: Standard gauge – 4 foot 8½ in. (1,435 mm).
Network Length: 47.25 miles (76.04 km).

Edinburgh Tram Routes 1950–56

Service 1, Route Colours Red/Blue

Corstorphine (Maybury)–Murrayfield–Haymarket–Princes Street–Bridges–Nicolson Street–Newington Station– Craigmillar Park–Liberton (top of Liberton Brae), withdrawn 28 March 1954.

Service 2, Route Colours Blue/Blue

Granton (Square)–Newhaven–Lindsay Road–North Junction Street–Great Junction Street–Leith Walk–York Place–George Street–Haymarket–Dalry Road–Gorgie Road–Stenhouse, withdrawn 14 December 1952.

Service 3, Route Colours Blue/White

Stenhouse–Gorgie Road–Dalry Road–Haymarket–Princes Street–Bridges–Nicolson Street–Newington Station, withdrawn 28 March 1953.

Service 4, Route Colours White/Blue

Slateford Road–Ardmillan Terrace–Dalry Road–Haymarket–Princes Street–York Place–London Road–Abbeyhill–Piershill (Northfield Broadway), withdrawn 2 May 1953.

Service 5, Route Colours White/Green

Morningside Station–Church Hill–Grange Road–Salisbury–Nicolson Street–Bridges–Leith Street–London Road–Abbeyhill–Piershill (Northfield Broadway), withdrawn 31 October 1954.

Service 6, Route Colours White/Red

Post Office–Bridges–Nicolson Street–Salisbury–Grange Road–Marchmont Road–Melville Drive–Tollcross–Lothian Road–Princes Street–Post Office (circular route both directions–Marchmont Circle), withdrawn 27 May 1956.

Service 7, Route Colours Red/Red

Stanley Road (Newhaven)–Newhaven Road–Ferry Road–Great Junction Street–Leith Walk–Leith Street–Bridges–Nicolson Street–Newington Station–Craigmillar Park–Liberton (top of Liberton Brae), withdrawn 11 March 1956.

Service 8, Route Colours Red/Yellow

Granton (Square)–Granton Road–Ferry Road–Inverleith Row–Canonmills–Broughton Street–Leith Street–Bridges–Nicolson Street–Newington Station, withdrawn 3 April 1955.

Service 9, Route Colours Yellow/Yellow

Granton (Square)–Granton Road–Ferry Road–Inverleith Row–Canonmills–Broughton Street–Leith Street–Princes Street–Lothian Road–Tollcross–Gilmour Place–Polwarth–Colinton Road–Firrhill–Colinton, withdrawn 23 October 1955.

Service 10, Route Colours White/Yellow

Bernard Street–Constitution Street–Leith Walk–Leith Street–Princes Street–Lothian Road–Tollcross – Gilmour Place–Polwarth–Colinton Road–Firrhill–Colinton withdrawn 23 October, 1955. (NB: From January 1954 Service 10 swapped northern termini with Service 16 and thus became: Granton (Square)–Granton Road–Ferry Road–Great Junction Street, then as before from Foot of Leith Walk).

Service 11, Route Colours Red/White
Stanley Road (Newhaven)–Newhaven Road–Pilrig Street–Leith Walk–Leith Street–Princes Street–Lothian Road–Tollcross–Bruntsfield Place–Morningside Road Station–Comiston Road–Fairmilehead, withdrawn 12 September 1956.

Service 12, Route Colours Yellow/Blue
Corstorphine (Maybury)–Murrayfield–Haymarket–Princes Street–Leith Street–Leith Walk–Duke Street–Hermitage Place–Seafield Road–Portobello–Joppa, withdrawn 11 June 1954.

Service 13, Route Colours White/Green
Granton (Square)–Newhaven–Lindsay Road–Commercial Street–Constitution Street–Leith Walk–Leith Street–Princess Street–Lothian Road–Tollcross–Bruntsfield Place–Church Hill–Grange Road–Salisbury–Nicolson Street–Bridges–Leith Street–Leith Walk–Pilrig Street–Ferry Road–Granton Road–Granton (circular route, double loop, one direction: see Service 14), withdrawn 17 June 1956.

Service 14, Route Colours Yellow/Green
Granton (Square)–Granton Road–Ferry Road–Pilrig Street–Leith Walk–Leith Street–Bridges–Nicolson Street–Salisbury–Grange Road–Church Hill–Bruntsfield Place–Tollcross–Lothian Road–Princes Street–Leith Street–Leith Walk–Constitution Street–Commercial Street–Lindsay Road–Newhaven–Granton (circular route, double loop, one direction: see Service 13), withdrawn 17 June 1956.

Service 15, Route Colours Green/White
King's Road – Portobello Road – London Road – York Place – Princess Street – Lothian Road – Tollcross – Bruntsfield Place – Morningside Road – Comiston Road – Fairmilehead – (withdrawn 19 September 1954)

Service 16, Route Colours Green/Green
Granton (Square) – Granton Road – Ferry Road – Great Junction Street – Leith Walk – York Place – Princes Street – Lothian Road – Tollcross – Bruntsfield Place – Morningside Road Station – Comiston Road – Fairmilehead – (withdrawn 12 September 1956)
(NB: From January 1954, Service 16 swapped northern termini with Service 10 and became: Bernard Street–Constitution Street, then as before from Foot Of Leith Walk; when Services 13/14 were withdrawn in June 1956, Service 16, for the final 3 months, returned to Granton but this time via Newhaven)

Service 17, Route Colours White/White
Granton Square–Newhaven–Lindsay Road–Commercial Street–Constitution Street–Leith Walk–Leith Street–Bridges–Nicolson Street–Newington Station, withdrawn 11 March 1956.

Service 18, Route Colours Yellow/White
Waverley (south side of St. Andrew Square)–Princess Street–Lothian Road–Tollcross–Melville Drive–Clerk Street–Newington Station–Craigmillar Park–Liberton Dams, withdrawn 26 March 1950 – the first route to go but did not involve any track loss.

Service 19, Route Colours Green/Red
Craigentinny Avenue–Seafield Road–Hermitage Place–Duke Street–Leith Walk–Leith Street–Bridges–Nicolson Street–Melville Drive–Tollcross, withdrawn 27 May 1956.

Service 20, Route Colours Red/Red
Post Office–Regent Road–London Road–Portobello Road–Portobello–Joppa, withdrawn 13 November 1954.

Service 21, Route Colours Green/Green
Post Office–Regent Road–London Road–Portobello Road–Portobello–Joppa–Musselburgh–Levenhall, withdrawn 13 November 1954.

Service 22, Route Colours Blue/Blue
North Junction Street–Great Junction Street–Leith Walk–York Place–George Street–Haymarket–Dalry Road–Gorgie Road–Stenhouse, withdrawn 14 December 1952, in effect a short working of service 2.

Service 23, Route Colours Green/Yellow
Granton Road Station–Inverleith Row–Dundas Street–Hanover Street–Mound–George IV Bridge–Lauriston Place–Tollcross–Bruntsfield Place–Morningside Station. This was one of the last two routes to run until the final day, 16 November 1956.

Service 24, Route Colours Red/Red
Waverley (south side of St. Andrew Square)–Frederick Street–Circus Place–Stockbridge–Comely Bank (outbound via Princes Street and inbound via George Street), withdrawn 1 June 1952 – the first route to go which involved loss of track.

Service 25, Route Colours Blue/Yellow
Corstorphine (Maybury)–Murrayfield–Haymarket–Princess Street–York Place–Leith Walk–Duke Street–Hermitage Place–Seafield Road–King's Road (before August 1952 the western terminus was Drum Brae South), withdrawn 11 July 1954.

Service 26, Route Colours Blue/Red
Zoo Park–Murrayfield–Haymarket–Princes Street–Leith Street–London Road–Abbeyhill–Piershill (before August 1952 the western terminus was Drum Brae South), withdrawn 11 July 1954.

Service 27, Route Colours Yellow/Red
Granton Road Station–Inverleith Row–Dundas Street–Hanover Street–Mound–George IV Bridge–Lauriston Place–Tollcross–Gilmore Place–Polwarth–Colinton Road–Firrhill (after June 1954 the southern terminus became Craiglockhart), withdrawn 7 August 1955.

Service 28, Route Colours Blue/Green
Stanley Road (Newhaven)–Newhaven Road–Pilrig Street–Leith Walk–Leith Street–Princess Street–Lothian Road–Tollcross–Bruntsfield Place–Morningside Station–Comiston Road–Braids (introduced in 1946, the 28 was in effect a part day short working of route 11 but was one of the last 2 routes to run to the last day, 16 November 1956).

Horse-drawn tram at the GPO, turning into the Bridges from Princes Street, from a postcard.

Edinburgh and District Tramway Co. Ltd cable car No. 187 on route 3, Pilrig, Princes Street, Dalry and Gorgie, *c.* 1900.

Edinburgh and District Tramway Co. Ltd cable car is seen at the Comely Bank terminus *c.* 1915. Note the conductress which dates the photo to the First World War era, as women were only employed as 'clippies' for the duration of the war.

Edinburgh and District Tramway Co. Ltd double-deck cable car and crew are seen at Murrayfield *c.* 1914–18. Some cable cars received top deck covers from 1907, but many remained open topped till the electric era.

Edinburgh cable car No. 143 is seen at Goldenacre pre-1920. Apart from the type of shops the buildings remain the same today. The tram was one of the last six cars ordered by the Edinburgh Northern Company before the Edinburgh District Company took over the system.

Leith Corporation Tramways tram No. 6 is leaving Leith Depot on the official opening day of the system on 3 November, 1905, with Provost Mackie in charge. The first tram entered revenue service on 18 August, 1905.

Foot of Leith Walk with tram No. 23 on Service 7 to Liberton, 10 March, 1956. The Palace Cinema seen in the background is now a pub. Car 23 was supplied by English Electric of Preston in 1935, whilst car 260 was built by Metro-Cammell of Birmingham in 1933.

Edinburgh tram turning out of a busy Great Junction Street into Leith Walk.

Edinburgh tram No. 106 on Service 10 to Bernard Street is seen on a damp day travelling north in Constitution Street. The destination screen has been prematurely changed to 'Colinton' ready for the return journey.

Edinburgh tram No. 383 on Service 17 to Newington Station leaving Constitution Street (at the Foot of Leith Walk), 10 March, 1956. This was the last day of Service 17. Woolies' store is looking busy.

Edinburgh tram No. 54 on Service 16 to Granton at the Foot of Leith Walk, 11 September 1956 (last day). The Central Station and bar can be seen on the right of the picture.

Edinburgh tram No. 180, on Service 12 to Joppa, is seen heading down Leith Walk. The former Caledonian Railway 'Leith New Lines' bridge can be seen in the background. Car 180 was the experimental £4,000 tram built by the Corporation at Shrubhill Works in 1932.

Edinburgh tram No. 251, on Service 19 to Tollcross, is seen in Leith Walk passing Leith Depot on 20 August 1954. Car 251 was one of ten supplied by R. Y. Pickerings of Kilmarnock in 1932. There is now a current tram 251 serving the City of Edinburgh, the new trams having the fleet Nos 251 to 277.

Edinburgh tram No. 359, on Service 17 to Newington Station, is seen passing Leith Depot on 10 March 1956, on the last day of this service.

Edinburgh tram No. 288 turning into Leith Depot; the Alhambra Theatre (opened 1914) is seen in the background, 3 April 1953. Note the conductor is carefully holding the trolley rope in case of de-wiring as the trolley pole is being pushed rather than trailing.

Edinburgh tram No. 107, on Service 9 to Colinton, proceeding up Leith Walk having just left Leith Depot.

Edinburgh streamliner tram No. 13 on Service 7 to Liberton, despite the destination screen saying Stanley Road, it is seen travelling up Leith Walk on 3 December 1955. Car 13 was supplied by Hurst Nelson of Motherwell in 1935.

Edinburgh tram No. 138, on Service 17 to Newington Station, passing Macdonald Road on the last day of service, 10 March 1956.

Edinburgh tram No. 252 passing a busy Elm Row–London Road. A Rankins' lorry can be seen delivering fruit and vegetables. Rankins had various shops spread throughout Leith and Edinburgh at this time.

Edinburgh tram No. 221, on Service 28 from Stanley Road to the Braids, is seen in Union Place with Bandparts and the Deep Sea chip shop in the background on 19 April 1954. Tram 221 was built at Shrubhill Works in 1939.

Edinburgh streamliner tram No. 17, on Service 11 to Stanley Road, is seen in Leith Street on 26 March 1955. The Playhouse Cinema can be seen in the background.

Edinburgh trams, Nos 159 and 166, on Service 9 to Granton and Colinton, are seen in Broughton Street–Picardy Place on 26 March 1955.

A 'Pram on a tram' can be seen on tram No. 104 on Service 8 to Newington Station at Broughton Street–Picardy Place. One woman passenger was heard to exclaim 'I hope the bairn's oot the pram!' Parcels etc. were often carried by trams, the Parcel Office being on Leith Walk at Shrubhill.

Edinburgh tram No. 182, on Service 8 to Granton, passing the Theatre Royal on 10 September 1953. The theatre burned down in 1946 and was not rebuilt due to a post-war shortage of building materials. This whole area was demolished to create a large traffic island.

Edinburgh tram No. 91 in Broughton Street–Picardy Place (enthusiast's special hire) on 10 April 1955. (See next picture regarding this seldom used connection.)

Tram No. 89, on a diverted Service 9 to Granton, is seen turning from York Place into Broughton Street. This is the same location as the last picture and was probably photographed during a parade along Princes Street that closed the road and caused temporary disruption to many tram services. The Service 11 tram in York Place and the 'blank' extra behind, both showing 'Post Office' on the destination, would in fact terminate in St Andrew Square until Princes St reopened.

Edinburgh tram No. 38, on Service 9 to Colinton, is seen picking up passengers in a very wet Leith Street on 6 April 1953.

Various trams and traffic are mixed together at the top of Leith Street. Trams were blamed for causing congestion, but clearly here public transport is being held up by other vehicles.

Edinburgh tram No. 333, on Service 14 to Churchhill, is seen turning into Princes Street at the top of Leith Street, date unknown.

Edinburgh tram No. 60, on Service 8 to Newington Station, is seen outside the GPO on 28 July 1952.

Edinburgh tram No. 164 turning into Princes Street from Leith Street, bound for Newington Station on 3 September 1955. 'Blank' route Numbers were used to indicate rush hour extras or part route services. Car 164 is one of the earlier Shrubhill domed roof Standard Cars of which eighty-four were built between 1934 and 1950.

After leaving, Leith Walk trams travelled either along Great Junction Street or Constitution Street to Granton. Edinburgh tram No. 266, on Service 17 to Granton, is seen in Constitution Street on 3 August 1953. Car 266, when new in 1930, was numbered 371 and for a few months ran on an experimental truck, later adopting the vacant fleet number of an ex-Leith Corporation tramcar which had been withdrawn. Thus until after the Second World War, when eleven trams were acquired second-hand from Manchester the highest fleet, it was No. 370.

Edinburgh tram No. 260 is seen in Bernard Street going towards Granton, despite the destination screen saying Fairmilehead, in June 1956. The tram will eventually go to Fairmilehead after reversing at Granton.

The Swing Bridge at Commercial Street, Leith, with Edinburgh tram No. 70 bound for Leith Depot.

Edinburgh tram No. 369 on Service 17 to Newington Station in Commercial Street crossing the railway tracks connecting the former North British Railway North Leith (Citadel) Station to Leith Docks. The Highland Queen whisky bond is now shops and flats. The station building still stands in Commercial Street.

Edinburgh tram No. 258, on Service 14 to Granton, is seen outside Leith North Station (ex-Caledonian Railway) at Hamburgh Place (Lindsay Road). This site is now flats and Ocean Terminal nearby is where the Royal Yacht *Britannia* is moored. Coincidentally, tram 258 of the new Edinburgh tram fleet was unfortunately involved in a serious accident near Edinburgh Airport and returned to Spain for repair.

Edinburgh tram No. 219, on Service 14 to Granton, is seen at Annfield (Lindsay Road) Newhaven. Ranks flour mill can be seen in the background.

Edinburgh experimental tram No. 180 of 1932, bound for the Foot of the Walk, is seen in Newhaven.

Edinburgh tram No. 76 on Service 16 to Granton, despite the destination screen saying Braids. It will eventually go to the Braids, passing under the bridge at Trinity Crescent (The Pinch) on 25 June 1956. A train with coal for Granton Gas Works is seen passing overhead.

Edinburgh tram No. 330 on Service 13 in Lower Granton Road, with the ex- North British Railway line to Granton on the right of the picture.

Edinburgh tram on Service 17 to Newington Station and a coal train are seen in Lower Granton Road on 3 August 1953. The locomotive is an ex-North British Railway J35 which lasted through the LNER era to the British Railways age.

Edinburgh tram No. 81 on Service 14 to Churchhill at Lower Granton Road, with the railway yard at Granton in the background.

Edinburgh tram No. 101, on Service 8 to Newington Station, is seen at Granton Square on 12 March 1955.

Edinburgh tram No. 265, on Service 13 to Churchhill, is seen at Granton Square. This rather bashed No. 265 is the sister car to No. 260 seen in previous pictures supplied by Met-Cam in 1933.

Edinburgh tram No. 167, on Service 9 to Colinton, is seen at Granton Square (BR loco No. 68340 is seen shunting in background).

Edinburgh trams 155, 217 and a bus on Service 17 to the West End via Muirhouse are seen waiting to depart Granton Square.

Edinburgh tram, on Service 9 to Colinton, is at the bottom of Granton Road with Granton Post Office in the background. Note the pram.

Edinburgh tram No. 119, on Service 9, is seen at Granton being made ready for the return journey to Colinton on 26 February 1955.

Edinburgh tram No. 242, on Service 14 to Churchhill, is seen at the bottom of Granton Road passing Wardie Steps. Car 242 was one of six all-steel trams supplied by Met-Cam of Birmingham in 1934 which were beset with corrosion problems, with one scrapped as early as 1950. 242 was the last survivor until June 1955 and often used on the Granton Circle Services 13 and 14.

Edinburgh tram No. 186, on Service 8 going to Granton, is seen at the corner of Fraser Avenue–Granton Road.

Edinburgh tram 158 and 312, on Services 27 to Firrhill and 14 to Churchhill, are seen outside Granton Road Station (ex-Caledonian Railway) on 3 August 1953.

Edinburgh tram No. 164, on Service 23, is seen turning from Ferry Road into the terminus at the top of Granton Road on 3 August 1953.

Edinburgh tram No. 202 at the corner of Granton Road and Ferry Road. Wardie Garage, now demolished, can be seen in the background. Looks like some road works are being carried out.

Edinburgh tram No. 57, on Service 9 to Granton, is seen turning into Ferry Road at Goldenacre. Note the lack of traffic lights.

Edinburgh tram No. 75 on Service 23 at Goldenacre on 11 October 1954.

Edinburgh tram No. 52, on Service 23 to Morningside Road Station, is seen in Inverleith Row on 1 September 1956. Heriots RFC stand can be seen in the background.

Edinburgh tram No. 160, on Service 9, is seen in Inverleith Row and will soon pass the entrance to the Royal Botanic Garden Edinburgh on its way to Colinton.

Edinburgh streamliner tram No. 16, on Service 23 to Morningside Road Station, is seen at Canonmills. The building in the background has recently been demolished for redevelopment.

Edinburgh tram, on Service 27 from Firrhill to Granton Road Station, is seen turning into Howard Place from Canonmills on 3 August 1953.

Edinburgh tram No. 268 is seen travelling down Brandon Terrace on Service 23 to Granton Road Station.

Edinburgh tram No. 231 to Liberton is seen at the terminus of Service 7 at the bottom of Craighall Road. Masons bakery shop, famous for its pies, is still in existence. Despite the advert on the side of the tram for Edinburgh Zoo, Service 7 didn't go anywhere near Edinburgh Zoo. Car 231 was one of three supplied by Hurst Nelson of Motherwell in 1934. Not many passengers would notice the detail differences to the 84 Shrubhill domed roof cars of very similar appearance!

Edinburgh tram No. 37, on Service 11 to Fairmilehead, is seen travelling up Craighall Road on 11 September 1956, the last day.

Edinburgh tram No. 148, on Service 28 to the Braids, is seen in Stanley Road about to turn into Newhaven Road, known locally as 'Cherry Bank Corner'.

Edinburgh tram No. 239, on Service 11, is seen at Newhaven Road, crossing Ferry Road Junction on its way to Fairmilehead via Pilrig Street. Car 239 is a sister car to 231 (see page 37).

Edinburgh tram No. 225, on Service 14 to Churchhill, is seen at Bonnington Toll. The ex-Caledonian Railway girder bridge carrying the line to South Leith has long since been demolished.

The rear entrance to Shrubhill was reached by a single track from Pilrig Street along Dryden Street. Edinburgh streamliner tram No. 11 (Hurst Nelson 1935) is seen travelling up Dryden Street heading back to Shrubhill Depot. This track was built after the amalgamation of Edinburgh and Leith tramways and the electrification of the Edinburgh system in 1922.

Edinburgh tram No. 107, on Service 28 to the Braids, is seen in Pilrig Street. Pilrig Street was where crews changed, as can be seen from the men sitting on the bench outside Pilrig Church.

Edinburgh trams 250 and 262 are seen in Pilrig Street. Note the coal lorry, now a thing of the past. Car 262 was one of three streamliners supplied in 1934 by English Electric of Preston (twenty further similar cars were supplied the following year by three outside builders).

Edinburgh tram No. 40 (built 1937) at Shrubhill with the Halfway House pub in the background.

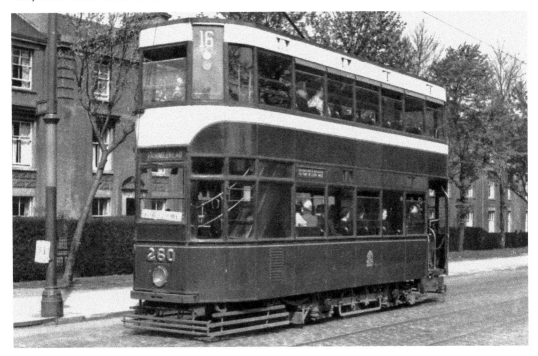

Edinburgh tram No. 260, on Service 16 to Fairmilehead, is seen travelling along Ferry Road. This picture dates from pre-summer of 1952 as the tram does not have advertising on the side.

Edinburgh tram No. 242 to Churchhill, passing the site of the ex- Caledonian Railway's Ferry Road Station on their ill-fated 'Leith New Lines'. This station was never opened to fare-paying passengers. The site became Pratt Bros, an electrical business, and is now flats.

Edinburgh tram No. 227, on Service 7 to Stanley Road, is seen in a deserted Ferry Road on 10 March 1956, last day.

Edinburgh tram No. 247, on Service 7 to Stanley Road, is seen at Junction Bridge on 10 March 1956, last day. The State Cinema can be seen to the left of the picture.

Edinburgh tram No. 166, on Service 12 to Corstorphine, is seen in Duke Street on 8 August 1953.

Edinburgh tram No. 170 on Service 19 to Tollcross is seen in Duke Street on 3 August 1953. The Palace Cinema, now a pub, is seen on the left of the picture.

Edinburgh tram, on Service 25 to Corstorphine, is seen on the single track in Duke Street on 10 September 1953. The sign for Glover Street can be seen on the building wall in the background.

Edinburgh tram No. 316, with a full load, is on Service 12 to Corstorphine, standing outside the NB Hotel, Princes Street, on 30 July 1950. Despite being renamed the 'Balmoral' (for the benefit of tourists) local residents still refer to the hotel as the 'NB'.

Edinburgh tram No. 213, on Service 28 to the Braids via the Mound and Tollcross, seen in Princes Street on 16 November 1956, last day. From mid-September 1956 to the end, Service 28 was diverted to run via the Mound to allow track lifting in west Princes Street and Lothian Road.

Edinburgh tram No. 367 in Princes Street, on Service 11 to the Braids.

Edinburgh tram No. 367, on Service 11 to Fairmilehead, passing the North British & Mercantile Insurance Building in Princes Street.

An old picture of Edinburgh trams in a very busy Princes Street at the bottom of the Mound with a tram for Piershill in the foreground c. 1933. Note the older livery on the upper decks which was superseded in the mid-1930s; also car No. 70, which appears in post-Second World War paint style on page 26.

Edinburgh tram No. 32 turning off Princes Street at Hanover Street bound for Granton Road Station, despite what the destination screen says, on 6 September 1956.

Edinburgh tram No. 85 on Service 23, entering Hanover Street having descended The Mound and crossed Princes Street bound for Granton Road Station, 28 August 1954. Note the 'Thorntons' sports shop on the corner which closed many years ago and is now a jeweller's shop.

Edinburgh tram on Service 23 to Morningside Station at the bottom of Hanover Street, July 1956. Note the 'Brown Derby' restaurant which offered 3/6d lunches at that time!

Edinburgh tram No. 307, on Service 27 to Granton Road Station, at the Mound–Princes Street on a wet 5 April 1953. The policeman on point duty must have been very unhappy having to stand there in such weather.

A selection of Edinburgh trams are seen in Princes Street in July 1956.

Edinburgh tram No. 72 (built 1941) bound for Granton, is seen in Princes Street on 30 April 1955, when cars were allowed to park in Princes Street.

Edinburgh tram No. 210, on Service 16 to Granton, is seen in Princes Street in July 1956. Preparatory work is already evident for track-lifting after services 11 and 16 would be withdrawn in September 1956.

Edinburgh tram No. 145, on Service 16 to the Braids, at the West End of Edinburgh where some sort of parade looks like it is about to start, July 1956. All the shops including the bank are now gone.

Edinburgh tram No. 119, on Service 9, is seen at the West End. Looking at the drawn blinds in the shops and deserted streets it would appear the picture was taken on a Sunday.

Edinburgh tram No. 106 (Peak hour Extra) is seen in Shandwick Place. The building next to the West End Café ('the Wec') is the former Albert Hall cinema.

Edinburgh tram No. 321, on Service 26 to Piershill, is seen in West Maitland Street. The clock/bell tower of St George's West church can be seen in the background surrounded by scaffolding.

Edinburgh tram No. 265 to Corstorphine (Zoo Extra) is seen crossing Haymarket Junction. Note the driver with a white topped cap, worn for the summertime.

Edinburgh tram No. 347 outside Haymarket Station in 1955. The restaurant in the background was demolished to make way for Edinburgh's new trams. The station was for a short time the terminus station on the Edinburgh and Glasgow Railway prior to the Haymarket tunnel being built.

Edinburgh tram No. 177, on Service 4 to Slateford, is seen in Dalry Road passing Dalry Cemetery.

Edinburgh tram No. 153 standing outside Gorgie Depot, 5 April 1953. The rear gardens of the tenements in Westfield Road were very small.

Edinburgh tram No. 184, on Service 4 to Slateford, is seen at Ardmillan Junction. Note the poor condition of the track, which resulted in the Gorgie and Slateford services being withdrawn by May 1953.

Edinburgh tram No. 58, on Service 4, is seen turning at Ardmillan Terrace into Slateford Road for the journey to the terminus outside Slateford Station.

Edinburgh tram No. 189 on Service 4 in Slateford Road travelling westbound towards Slateford terminus on 6 April 1953 (the destination has already been changed for the return journey). The tram is passing Gorgie East Station on the Suburban Line and Bernards Brewery.

Edinburgh tram No. 166, on Service 4 to Piershill, at Slateford terminus outside Slateford Station on 6 April 1953.

Edinburgh tram No. 38, bound for Zoo Park, is seen at Roseburn passing under the ex-Caledonian Railway bridge carrying the line to Leith North Station. The bridge still exists and the former railway line is now a walkway.

Edinburgh tram No. 169 on Service 12 to Corstorphine at Zoo Park (169 was the last car from Corstorphine).

Three Edinburgh trams – 107, 411 and 77 – are seen at Zoo Park on 18 April, 1954. Note the loop line to park extra trams at busy times. Car 411 is one of the eleven purchased from Manchester Corporation between 1947 and 1949 and were normally restricted to the Portobello and Musselburgh routes due to being longer than the other cars, creating concerns over clearance at sharp bends. Car 411 had been chartered by an enthusiasts' group, hence its presence on the Corstorphine line.

Edinburgh tram No. 316, on Service 25, is seen in St Johns Road, Corstorphine, on 18 October 1953. The garage in the background has since been demolished.

Edinburgh tram No. 182, on Service 25 in St John's Road, heading west on 19 April 1954.

Edinburgh tram No. 246, on Service 12 to Joppa, is seen at the terminus outside the Maybury Garage on the Glasgow Road. This was one of six trams supplied by Met-Cam in 1934 which suffered from corrosion and was withdrawn in June 1952, so never received adverts.

The Lothian Road subway entrance to Princes Street (ex-Caledonian Railway) Station, with Edinburgh tram No. 62, on Service 6, 'Marchmont Circle', in the foreground, 26 March 1955.

Edinburgh tram No. 63 is seen travelling down Lothian Road. The ex-Caledonian Railway goods yard on the left is now the West Approach Road.

Edinburgh tram No. 52, bound for Fairmilehead, is seen in Lothian Road on 11 September 1956.

Edinburgh tram No. 88 travelling up Lothian Road en route to Colinton.

Edinburgh tram No. 146, outside Tollcross depot about to go on Service 27 to Granton Road Station. This was a former cable car depot and power station and a new entrance was created for the electric trams (the cable car door was in the centre of the façade).

Edinburgh tram No. 62, on Service 6, is seen at Tollcross on 26 May 1956, last day.

Edinburgh trams 216 and 52, with a third tram just behind, are seen in Tollcross.

A very tranquil and peaceful Bruntsfield Place, with Edinburgh tram No. 153, on Service 13 to Churchhill, on 11 August 1953. The spire belongs to the Barclay Church.

Edinburgh tram No. 82, on Service 16 to the Braids, approaching the top of Bruntsfield Place on 1 September 1956.

Edinburgh tram No. 182, on Service 23 to Granton Road Station (passing Merchiston Place siding), 11 August 1953.

Edinburgh tram No. 180, the experimental modern car of 1932, built at a cost of £4,000, passes Holy Corner, Morningside. This tram was known as 'red biddy' due to its original colour, which resembled red wine.

Edinburgh tram No. 54, on Service 5, displaying the wrong destination screen, is seen turning out of Church Hill into Morningside Road heading to the terminus at Morningside Road Station. The tram will return to Piershill.

Edinburgh tram No. 80 on Service 23 outside Morningside Road Station.

Edinburgh tram No. 282, on Service 23 to Granton Road Station, is seen at the junction at Morningside Road Station.

Edinburgh tram No. 88 at the Braids Terminus on 26 September 1956. Note the 'pan' on the overhead, provided at each terminal during the war time to make rewiring the trolley easier in the blackout, but retained to the end as proved very useful.

Edinburgh tram No. 14, on Service 16 to Fairmilehead, is nearing the Braids on 24 April 1953.

Edinburgh tram No. 204, on Service 27 to Craiglockhart, is seen turning into Gilmour Place on 26 February 1955. Service 27 terminated at Firrhill for most of its life but latterly was, for a few months, curtailed to Polworth but re-extended to Craiglockhart till the end in August 1955.

Edinburgh tram No. 155, on Service 9 to Colinton, is about to enter the single track section in Gilmour Place on 12 September 1953. The King's Theatre can be seen in the background. This narrow bit of street was widened after the trams stopped.

Edinburgh tram No. 148, on Service 10 to Bernard Street, and No. 308, on Service 27 to Firrhill, pass each other in Granville Terrace on 11 August 1953. Note how near to the kerb the outbound track is here.

Edinburgh tram No. 330, on Service 27 to Granton Road Station, is seen on Colinton Road passing the top of Craiglockhart Avenue, 24 May 1953.

Edinburgh tram No. 177, on Service 9 from Granton to Colinton passing Merchiston Castle School on 12 March 1955. Another single track section where the road was widened afterwards.

Edinburgh tram No. 180, on Service 10 from Colinton to Granton, is seen outside Merchiston Castle School on 12 March 1954. The route of the 10s was altered from Bernard Street to Granton via Ferry Road in January 1954.

Edinburgh tram No. 155 for Granton is at the Colinton terminus, 22 October 1955. This was the last day of the Colinton Routes 9 and 10.

Colinton Terminus on the last day, 22 October 1955.

Post Office (GPO)–Waverley Station–Nicolson Street–Grange Road–Melville Drive–Tollcross–Lothian Road–Princes Street–GPO (circular route both directions–Marchmont Circle, Service 6)

Edinburgh tram No. 40, on Service 6, is seen in Princes Street on 30 April 1955. This route was the only truly circular tram route in Edinburgh.

Edinburgh tram No. 69, on Service 6, is seen in Marchmont Road, 26 May 1956. Car 69 was the prototype 'domed roof standard tram', built in Shrubhill works in late 1934, a further eighty-three followed between 1935 and 1950.

Edinburgh tram No. 56, on Service 6, 'Marchmont Circle', passing the Meadows on 26 May 1956 (last day) complete with police escort!

Edinburgh tram No. 119 on Service 5 in Beaufort Road at the junction with Marchmont Road.

The terminus of Service 24 was in Craigleith Road as seen on 15 August 1950. This route was the first to be abandoned involving loss of track mileage in 1952. The tram is No. 280 built in 1923 and from Tollcross Depot which serviced the former cable routes of the original Edinburgh Northern Company on the steep hills to the north of the New Town.

Edinburgh tram on Service 24, Comely Bank to Waverley, is seen in Stockbridge about to cross the bridge over the Water of Leith. The first cable car depot was in Henderson Row, off to the left of the picture.

Edinburgh tram No. 32, on Service 24 to Waverley, is seen at north-west Circus Place.

Edinburgh tram No. 117, on Service 24 to Waverley, turning from Frederick Street into George Street on 31 May 1952, last day.

Edinburgh tram No. 137 on Service 6, 'Marchmont Circle', is seen at the Post Office (GPO)–North Bridge.

Unknown Edinburgh tram is seen travelling over North Bridge.

This mid-1930s photo shows Edinburgh tram No. 63, on Service 8 to Newington Station, in North Bridge. This car is an electrified former cable car withdrawn in 1937 and replaced by a Shrubhill built tram in 1938.

Edinburgh tram No. 173 in seen passing Patrick Thomson Ltd store on 26 March 1955. Note the parked cars and ice cream van.

Edinburgh tram No. 201, on Service 17 to Newington Station, seen in South Bridge on 12 March 1955.

Edinburgh tram No. 39 on Service 19 to Tollcross in South Bridge, 26 May 1956, last day.

Edinburgh tram No. 111, on Service 6, 'Marchmont Circle', at Surgeon's Hall, 26 March 1955. As can be seen from the picture this was a very busy service. Car 111 was nicknamed 'Nelson' by crews at Portobello Depot where it spent most of its life being transferred to Tollcross Depot on closure of the Portobello routes in 1954.

Edinburgh tram No. 104, on Service 17 to Granton from Newington Station, is seen at last stop in Clerk Street with Nicholson Street beyond the traffic lights.

Edinburgh tram No. 265, on Service 19 to Tollcross, is seen turning at Clerk Street–Hope Park Terrace on 26 May 1956 (last day).

Edinburgh tram No. 77, on Service 17 to Granton, is seen in Newington Road at the Salisbury Place junction on 25 May 1953.

Edinburgh tram, on Service No. 17 route to Granton, is seen leaving Newington Station.

Edinburgh tram No. 304 on Service 17, outside the ex-North British Railway's Newington Station on Edinburgh's Suburban line. The streamliner is on service 7 to Stanley Road heading north in Mayfield Gardens on a rather misty day.

Edinburgh tram No. 54 of 1940 for Portobello is seen in Waterloo Place with several anxious passengers looking on.

Edinburgh tram No. 168 (to Musselburgh Town Hall) is seen passing the old Royal High School in Regent Road on 23 May 1953. Sadly, the trees on the right of the picture have been removed and in their place are car parking spaces.

Edinburgh tram No. 261, foreground, on Service 5 to Piershill, is seen in London Road at the top at Easter Road. The conductor of the tram seems to be having a discussion about something. Car 251 was a 'one off' Shrubhill product, having a modern car interior but a traditional 'wooden' style exterior, built 1933.

Edinburgh trams, numbers 119 and 111, are seen at Abbeyhill Junction on 2 August 1953. The former Trustee Savings Bank is on the right.

Edinburgh tram No. 168, on Service 20 to Joppa, is seen in London Road (Abbeyhill), 2 August 1953. Munro & Miller's Foundry is seen on the right of the picture.

Edinburgh tram No. 404, on Service 21 to the Post Office (GPO), is seen at Meadowbank. The area to the right is where the 1970 Commonwealth Games were held. Meadowbank Stadium and Leisure Centre is being redeveloped. Also at Meadowbank was St. Margarets Engine Sheds (ex-NBR), now an art studio and offices. Car 404, ex-Manchester 125, purchased 1947, was only used on Portobello routes.

Edinburgh tram No. 90, on Service 20 to Joppa, is seen passing Piershill Cemetery on Portobello Road on 6 April 1953.

Edinburgh tram No. 19 (English Electric 1935) on Service 12 to Corstorphine in King's Road. The power station is just visible behind the brewery lorry.

Edinburgh tram No. 162 on Service 21 to the Post Office (GPO) outside the George Cinema in Portobello, 23 May 1953.

Edinburgh tram No. 37 (built 1949), on Service 19 to Tollcross, is seen in Craigentinny Avenue.

Edinburgh streamliner tram No. 19 (again!), on Service 12 to Joppa, at Fillyside Road.

Edinburgh tram, on Service 21 to the Post Office (GPO), is seen in Musselburgh Road, Joppa, 19 April 1954. A wonderful atmospheric photograph with the Firth of Forth in the background. Car 410, ex-Manchester 349, purchased 1949, withdrawn 1954.

Edinburgh tram 174, on Service 21 to the Post Office (GPO), is seen in Fisherrow, Musselburgh, with the Ship Inn in the background. The wooden board on the front states that the tram goes to and from Portobello Beach and Pool. The open air pool at Portobello has long since been closed.

Edinburgh tram No. 161 is seen in Musselburgh High Street going to the Post Office (GPO).

Edinburgh tram No. 338 in Linkfield Road Musselburgh on race day. This tram is for the Post Office (GPO). The tram driver appears to be watching the horse racing, perhaps he has money on the favourite.

Edinburgh tram No. 101 entering Leith Depot from Leith Walk.

Edinburgh trams at both entrances to Leith Depot. The building in the middle, which housed the canteen and offices, has been refurbished while the tram/bus depot itself has been demolished for redevelopment.

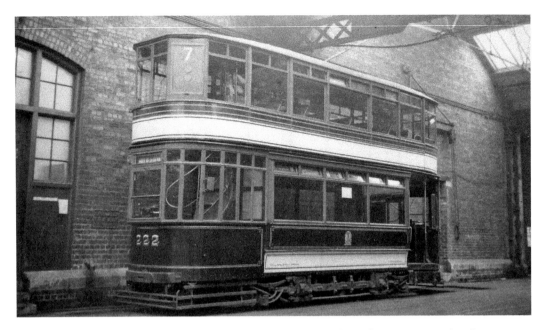

Former Edinburgh cable tram No. 222, on Service 7, is seen inside Leith Depot in 1920/30s livery. This tram was the only car in cable days to be fully enclosed earning the nickname 'Crystal Palace'. Note the unique split upper-deck windscreen. This tram was withdrawn 1938, but its 1938 replacement retained the nickname!

Edinburgh tram No. 79 outside Portobello Tram Depot. It would appear from the picture that tram enthusiasts were welcome. This former cable car depot was very congested with the main doors right at the footpath of Portobello High Street.

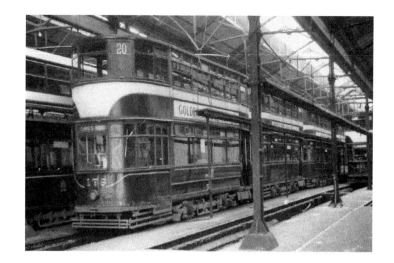

The interior of Portobello Tram Depot with quite a collection trams.

Interior of Shrubhill Depot and Works with service cars being kept there as a running depot from time to time. Car 50 was one of those built in 1950 and thus only had six years' service.

Edinburgh trams 62 and 75, among others, are seen in Tollcross Depot on 20 April 1954. This north part of the depot was formerly the power house driving the cable system in the south-west area of the city.

Edinburgh tram No. 31 is seen being guided into Tollcross Depot. The depot was demolished to make way for a new fire station. The old canteen building still exists and was, at one time, the home of Edinburgh Corporation Transport Boxing Club, which my father ran. It is now used for martial arts.

Edinburgh trams 315 and 302, on Services 2 and 3, are seen at Gorgie Depot. This depot was built new for the electric era but was the first to close in May 1953.

CITY AND ROYAL BURGH OF EDINBURGH
TRANSPORT DEPARTMENT

OPERATION OF LAST TRAM,
Friday, 16th November 1956.

This card is available on Reserved Car

No. *1* from Braids at *7.20* p.m.

W. M. LITTLE,
Transport Manager.

61—11/56

Car No. 88

Operation of Last Tram official ticket for tram No. 88 from the Braids.

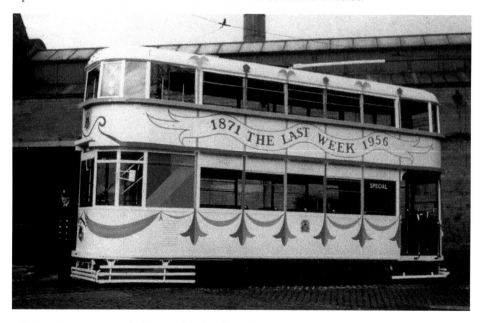

Edinburgh tram No. 172 (in 'last week' white livery), 14 November 1956. This car was new in 1950.

Edinburgh tram No. 172 is seen on The Mound on 16 November 1956, last day.

Edinburgh tram No. 172 in Hanover Street on the final day, 16 November 1956.

Edinburgh tram No. 219 (built 1948), on Service 23 to Granton Road Station, is seen at Morningside Station at 6.15 pm on 16 November 1956, last day.

Edinburgh trams 172, 88 and 217, on the Final Run to Shrubhill, are seen preparing to depart from the Mound, together with a horse-drawn omnibus on Friday 16 November 1956, last day of operations.

Acknowledgements

I would like to thank the following and anyone else I may have missed for their assistance and use of their pictures featured in this book:

The late J. L. Stevenson (Senior)

J. L. Stevenson (Junior)

The late P. D. Hancock

The late George Fairley

W. D. Yuill Collection

Kenneth G. Williamson Collection

'Electrail Slides' – The Electric Railway Society

George Murray

With special thanks to George Murray for his historical input.

I would also like to dedicate the book to my wife, Marjorie.

Kenneth G. Williamson
Edinburgh